CHARM FOR CA

MILENA WILLIAMSON

Charm for Catching a Train

Milena Williamson

Green Bottle Press

First published in 2022
by Green Bottle Press
83 Grove Avenue
London N10 2AL
www.greenbottlepress.com

Cover image: Alamy stock photo
Cover design by Økvik Design
Typeset by CB editions, London
Printed in England by Imprint Digital, Exeter EX5 5HY

ISBN 978 1 910804 26 1

Contents

Stranger

Walking farther than I have been before brings me to Tomb Street.
I'm a stone's throw away from Royal Mail, but I don't know where

and it's early days in Belfast and I've not got mail from anyone.
It's as good a street as any for learning how to look left and listen –

how's tricks catch yerself on aye meet yous at the back of Boots
I'll run ye over sure I almost lost the run of myself lookin at him.

I stand there searching for something déjà vu.
To feel like I have been before in a place I have never been

is all I can ask of this here city built on *wait until the green man*
shows opposite the north is next to let give way no ball games.

Feeling grows familiar as I peel a tangerine to smithereens.
I turn again into Tomb Street – *private gate keep clear*

queue here at any time on footway no persons beyond this point.
The inner ring does my head in as I follow it round and exit too early.

I call my father across the ocean and say *bout ye are you there*
ach sure ye know yerself can you hear me *right I'm away home.*

When We Meet

I am doing a handstand. Pressing green
palms to earth, I lunge with my head bent down
then fling my legs. You remove your glasses,
laying them down next to mine in the grass.

You stretch your shoulders then ask if my name
is spelled like Kafka's lover's. *Yes, it is.*
My mother studied Kafka while pregnant:
talking to the typewriter & my heartbeat
sliding the carriage as she finishes
a line, searching for syllables to shape

a daughter. We balance at the tipping
point where our names might revert to verbs.
If we can hold still for just a little
longer, the letters will descend like birds.

Love

adapted from the NHS page on pneumonia

It's more widespread in winter.
Symptoms can develop suddenly
or they may come on more slowly.
Your GP may listen to your chest
and check for crackling or rattling.
Are you breathing faster than usual?
Do you feel breathless even when resting?
Do you feel confused or disoriented?

Most cases can't be passed between people.
Mild cases can be treated at home.
It's usually safe for an infected person
to be around friends or family members.
It can affect anyone, but it's more serious
for the very young and the elderly.

He Calls and I Ring Him Back

My father trips during his morning run,
falls on the sidewalk and scrapes his knees.
He picks himself up, the damp leaves
clinging, the slip and salve of autumn.

Again my father stumbles on the pavement.
Embarrassed and covered in plasters,
he calls. I ring him back. I do not ask or
want to know how, only how many – silent

counting either end of the line, both sides
of the ocean so – thirteen Band-Aids.
Tomorrow he will walk around the block
or down the street. I would hold him back
if I were nearer and sitting in the shade
as my words leaf from his on this raw day.

How to Make Latkes in Belfast

Use Yukon Gold or Idaho,
my mother writes in her letter.
You can find them anywhere but
maybe they have another name.
Review miracles. Don't measure.
Potatoes are surprisingly
acidic, so remember not
to grate your thumb. Pour the oil.
Drop the mixture into the pan.

An Irish Woman Travels to England

for the 161 women who travelled from Northern Ireland in 2021
and for the thousands who made the journey before them

I cross the Irish Sea imagining
the curve of your chin and your eyes opening,
adjusting to light. The world is initially
strange. Above the clouds, the atmosphere
thins. Darling, you have mastered mimicry.
You practice the art of breathing, swallowing
the yellowish liquid that cradles you, sampling
what feeds you, nutrient-rich. You imitate
the rise and fall of my lungs. It's difficult
to talk to you now. In the hospital
I will not sing. No more lullabies
until I feel the anaesthesia –
it arrives like a circus at night, stealthily
setting up tents and unlatching the animals
who claw at their costumes and howl as you
hang upside down on the red trapeze.

The Room

after 'Snow' by Louis MacNeice

I am looking at *Woman in a Tub* in the Tate shop online,
which is to say I am changing the frame, the matte,
the size of the print, the colour of the wall on which it hangs,
even the room, suddenly hers. She covers her breasts

above a bed spawning pillows, soundlessly inviting,
gets gooseflesh and fancies pulling the blanket –
possibly flannel, incompatible with the open window –
from where it's draped over one side of the bed.

There's no option to hang her in the bathroom,
but she's incorrigible, bathing in multiple living rooms.
She turns away from the roses whose colour I can't change
and washes an arm behind a table bearing oranges,

or tangerines, or clementines, or any otherwise
peach-coloured glass baubles that can't be peeled or pipped.
She steps out of the tub with a bubbling sound for world
and slips through the door, into more of it than we think.

Made in the USA

My brother and I count ten paces, both of us
with half a mind to turn and draw too soon

like Yosemite Sam bursting into the dusty saloon:
any one of you lily-livered, bow-legged varmints

care to slap leather with me? We are armed
with Silly String, the neighbours' half-used cans,

for there are no Nerf guns strewn across our lawn
and no yellow slugs in the flowerbeds.

Shake can thoroughly! Locate target and be silly!
Container may explode if heated!

My father burnt his draft card in his father's face.
We skip the camo aisle in Kids R Us.

Shoot to increase the happy atmosphere!
Do not hold can upside-down! Made in the USA!

My father can light a candle, lick his fingers
and pinch it out without the smallest sound.

Exposure to sunlight may cause can to burst!
Do not spray on face! Safe for children!

We flip our baseball caps with sticky fingers,
cool as Bugs Bunny eyeing the mobsters:

[Bang!] [Click click.] That's the trouble
with carrots, they're only good once.

My brother and I take turns being the baddie,
staring down the one we know so well.

Terminal Six

After exiting JFK, I hold my hand
out the cab window
and reach for the dark buildings.
From the mirror, dice
hang. The cabbie turns to my brother:
you look like a terrorist.

I think, *you look like a terrorist*
too. The cabbie drives with one hand.
Turning to my brother,
I catch his face in the window,
spilling like dice.
I reach for him in the dark as buildings

rear back. As kids, we reached for building
blocks and did not look like terrorists
when we knocked the towers down. A roll of the dice –
our small hands
might shake then the roofs and windows
would crumple. On lucky days, my brother

finished a tower, tall as he was. My brother
tears down and rebuilds
singing, *and their shoes were like windows,*
and their shoes were like bone. We terrorised
our cities, hand-
built from red blocks like diced

cubes of meat, but nobody died.
Nobody lived there but my brother
and me. It only looked a little like Manhattan.

Tonight, my brother faces the buildings.
The cabbie turns onto the highway, terrified
of the rain on the windows

and the rain on the roof as I wind
my watch back like a bomb. The dice
clack against each other like terrorists
tapping out codes. Looking out, my brother
uses his fingers to measure buildings.
The cabbie swings one arm, the hand

of a speeding clock. The buildings on our street reach for my hand.
The cabbie turns in the terrible dark then turns against my brother.
My brother's eyes are dice in the reflection in the window.

The Wolf

Upon arriving at Ellis Island, my great-grandmother and her children are stopped by an immigration inspector. What are you carrying? Where are you going? Who are you meeting? He peels back their eyelids and asks them to open wide.

In the tenements, my granny shares a bed with her sisters. The next morning, she turns a dial on the gas stove and a stranger slaps her hand. His nails are too long. His mouth is too big. In New York City, my granny has forgotten her father's face. In New York City, the buildings shine like teeth.

In one version, an ogress eats the grandmother. She stews her teeth and fries her ears. The ogress watches her womanly figure. This tale takes place beside the Jordan River. I have floated in the mouth of this river, the Dead Sea holding me. The water parts for the girl and drowns the ogress.

Parkinson's knocks on my granny's door and speaks with a voice like my own. Granny says I am not Jewish enough. I want to slit her stomach and fill her with stones. In Judaism, the tradition of placing stones on graves came from the need to prevent wild animals from devouring bodies.

Sometimes, the wolf only swallows a mouthful of dark red cloth and it burns his throat. My mother puts granny in my bed. We light the Chanukah candles. I hold the match to the wick and linger. Wax drips on my hand. My mother sings, rubbing aloe on my skin. She sings herself hoarse.

Alone in Prague, I tour the Old Jewish Cemetery, where no one can be buried now. The tour guide says that if a leaf falls and grazes your cheek, you have to bathe to wash the dead from your body. Sometimes, the girl throws her clothes into the fire and gets into bed with the wolf.

Entry

Rifling through my father's journal,
I find sums in the margins, reports labelled

not for publication, quotes from Rilke,
scribbled poems, a recipe for griddlecakes,

a sketch of a woman, a blue airmail
slip unaddressed and not one detail

of what he said to the local draft board,
his objection to war on the record.

He shaved his face to the quick.
A white handkerchief in his pocket.

Three men assessed his belief in God
or a being who otherwise occupied

a place parallel: yes sir, no sir.
My father did not become a soldier.

The Outing

Did we travel on the north-south yellow
or east-west red? Apart or together
every day we played spot-the-most-tortured
security guard, saint or gargoyle.

Out of season, we tried a winter dish
of pomegranates, the one that translates
to beneath a snowy white carpet. It's
a carpet better shared with you. I wish

we had more souvenirs – an evening gown,
a monogrammed hairbrush, a nameless round
of hide and seek in the balcony room.
The blue canopy bed, an open tomb.

Let's buy walking sticks for when we are women
of another age, back home for teatime.

On Our Night Out

He gets the steak and I get the chicken.
The waiter lights a candle.

We discuss our dreams:
in mine, moles invade my old house

and they nibble my neck.
His dream has teeth in all the wrong places

and he won't even hold my hand in public.
We chew the tough meat.

My first cat died in that house –
I buried Catty out front under the cherry tree.

His milky eye was still open: a piece of fat
the moon spat back. *It was a rental.*

My second cat died of shock
when I told him I fell

in love with a married man. Nobody
recorded the time of death. Tenderly

I fold my napkin
like a burning house.

How They Kept Their Wings: a Triptych

Life	Time	Line
reminds me	to lock	up the forks and knives
once	the doors	set
emergency	fires	the table
was a body	stoked	like shrapnel
rising from a body	the man	the planes
of water	and the woman	all degenerated
how	they kept their	wings
almost every	house	became windows
culture	the children	the fuselage
has a flood	in bed	the plane's
myth	said	everything truly
this suggests	once upon a	spindle
a flood or	time there was the	body
the need for	closing	fathers and mothers
one	passage	forks
for some	once upon	knives and passengers

Fathom

Because his hut overlooks the village path,
he bathes at night. I hold my breath
as he strikes a match and lights the kerosene
in the lamp made from a tin of margarine.

In this corner, a bucket for washing, my father
writes before he sheds his clothes to fathom
the water he has carried from the river, home.
He unfolds a towel and I turn hereafter –

I draw my own bath to feel a little closer
in a city at the mouth of another river.
I extend a hand to test the water

against my wrist as if I could reach him.
I loop my loved one's lines and listen
for the purling sound as he steps in.

On Our Last Night in Lancaster, Pennsylvania

I touch your knee. We leave the bar early,
but as we walk you realise your card
is gone. We loop back –
                                    the construction paused
on the street, the closed Amish bakery
where the woman who opened the oven
wore a white bonnet, stiff as a dead dove,
where we ate pastries. We watch a car drive
past a horse-drawn carriage, moving over
into the opposite lane, a wide berth
since horses on the road spook easily.
Each driver looks up from his century
towards the other –
                              At the bar, you hurry
inside while I wait by the door. I shoot
you a loving glance. It's still not too late.

Ghosts

I crush eggshells into confetti for the compost
and my father stops humming to scrape his plate
and say *I had a friend and he made a pass at me.*

A pass as if they were both trying to catch a fly ball,
the sun in their eyes as they ran and maybe the boy
lay a little too long in the grass after they collided.

My father doesn't like the look of runny eggs,
not since he had amoebic dysentery years ago
and I know home by the overcooked smell.

He turns on the tap and never says the boy's name.
I ask about class. He's teaching *Hamlet* tomorrow:
If thou has any sound, or use of voice, speak to me,

I say as Horatio, calling Hamlet's father's ghost.
Before we say goodnight, I stack books beneath his bed
in order to send the stomach acid farther from his throat.
What can I do but lift my father's bed while I am here.

Someone

My mother dusts the portraits on her desk:
my brother wears her glasses upside-down,
owl-eyed with whimsy; I'm in the yellow dress

patterned with teapots, grape jelly on my cheeks;
my father smiles at the end of the aisle, his luck
to find someone who writes and roller-skates;

my grandparents, their arms almost touching,
their backs to the river of some American city;
their own cousins in razed European towns;

my mother, draped in green, sitting alone –
eyes closed, mouth open – leaning into light.
I know her and I have never known her.

Untitled Nude

for E

No space must be regarded as great except the ocean. – Edgar Degas

Do not forget that the exhibition is only two steps from the street corner.
– J. M. Michel

Once the space between us was as great as the ocean.
Now we sit close, eat mocha cheesecake at midnight,
sleep late and kiss goodbye, lingering on the street corner.

You ask if I lived an alternate life before we met.
I fall into the multiverse of girl-body-person-woman
with every text, floating or drowning between oceans

and yes, I have been catcalled. On the street, on the corner,
once, braless and running to Victoria Square for lingerie.
Afterwards, in a blue dress, I read poems in The American.

I do not want to be regarded by anyone except the ocean:
Barleycove, Coral Beach, Rosses Point, Kinnagoe Bay.
In Blackhead, we walk past the lighthouse, down the stairs

and sit on the rocks, eating steak pasties in the salty air.
The life with you is the one in which I am healed;
you kneel on a towel and I sit on the bathtub's corner.

Afterwards, I stand at the window in the dark kitchen
to drink water, eat a yogurt and fix my hair, still nude.
At every corner, I am a woman on a street corner.
Regarding myself (as you do), I am as great as the ocean.

Charm for Catching a Train

I buy a return and say she wants the same.
The man gives her an accidental discount,
a kind of love, and she fumbles with the coins.
Without touching, I show her what she needs
and the exact change passes between our palms.
I take her by the elbow and through the gates
before we trade to-go cups to stir and wonder
how the vanilla is more aftertaste than taste.

This also might be love. At the end of the line,
we will find the castle and boats setting sail.
She asks how to alight, whether people
go one at a time or everyone alights together.
The platform number is days spent in love.
A train arrives from the right direction.

ACKNOWLEDGEMENTS

Thanks to the editors of the following journals in which some of these poems were first published: 'Stranger' in *Hold Open the Door* (the Ireland Chair of Poetry Commemorative Anthology 2020); 'When We Meet' and 'Terminal Six' in *Blackbird: New Writing from the Seamus Heaney Centre* volume two; 'Love' and 'On Our Last Night in Lancaster, Pennsylvania' in New Irish Writing in the *Irish Independent*; 'He Calls and I Ring Him Back' in *Poetry Ireland Review* issue 137; 'How to Make Latkes in Belfast' in *The North* issue sixty-one (the Irish Issue); 'An Irish Woman Travels to England' on Belfast's Poetry Jukebox, on RTÉ online and in the Poetry Ireland Introductions 2018 e-book; 'The Outing' in *Poetry Ireland Review* issue 126; 'On Our Night Out', which was commended in the *Magma Poetry* competition 2018/2019 and published in *Magma* online; 'How They Kept Their Wings: a Triptych' in *Oxford Poetry* issue ninety-two; 'Untitled Nude' in *Romance Options: Love Poems for Today*; 'Charm for Catching a Train' in *Washing Windows Too* (Irish Women Write Poetry).

The first epigraph of 'Untitled Nude' comes from *Degas Letters* edited by Marcel Guerin and translated from the French by Marguerite Kay. The second epigraph comes from J. M. Michel's critique of Degas's exhibition of pastels featuring nude women at their toilette. The form of this poem was inspired by Gail McConnell's 'Untitled/Villanelle'.

Thank you to everyone at the Seamus Heaney Centre, in particular Stephen Sexton, Fran Brearton, Gail McConnell, Leontia Flynn, Glenn Patterson and Rachel Brown. An extra thanks to Stephen, who supervised my MA and PhD, from which many of these poems are drawn. Thank you, Ciaran Carson, who welcomed me to Belfast and into Irish poetry. To everyone in Ciaran's workshop and in the Lemon Experiment. To Stephen Connolly and Manuela Moser, who gave some of these poems their first home in *The Lifeboat* reading series. To David Torrans and Claudia Edelmann for No Alibis Bookstore. To Paul Maddern for reading some of these poems at the

River Mill Writers' Retreat. To Shane McCrae, my undergraduate poetry professor. To Mimi Drew, my high school creative writing teacher. To Fiona Benson, Moyra Donaldson and Jessica Traynor, for their mentoring and encouragement. I am grateful for the support of the Arts Council of Northern Ireland. Thank you to the judges of the Mairtín Crawford Poetry Award in 2018. Thank you to the Society of Authors and the judges of the Eric Gregory Award in 2021. Thank you, Jennifer Grigg, for believing in these poems and for making my first pamphlet real.

Thank you to the Totten and McPhilemy families. To Ciara, for her kindness. To Jake, for his wisdom. To Jenna, Tory and Maria for supporting and challenging me. To Bebe, who made our wee house a home. To Marina, for being my oldest friend and braving Belfast rain. Thank you, Alyssa, for long walks in the Crum Woods and even longer letters. Thank you, Caden and Telory, for sisterly wisdom. Thank you, Sophie, for travel adventures and literary chats. Thank you, Marc, for floor-dancing and pomez bopo. Thank you, Mom and Dad, for loving me and believing in my poetry. You da bestest! An extra thanks to Dad for the line, 'And their shoes were like windows, and their shoes were like bone' and for answering all my questions. Thank you, Eoghan, my loving person. Thank you for reading and editing these poems and so many others. Thank you for coming down from the mountain in time (ish) for our first date and for all the mountains we will climb together. Guess what?